Let Me Help

by Lili Henderson
illustrated by Lesley Breen Withrow

I can help with the vase.

I can help with the cape.

I can help with the book.

4

I can help with the plane.

I can help with the dog.

I can help with the gate.

Can I help with the
sandwich, too?